The First Christmas

Copyright © 1981 by Our Sunday Visitor, Inc.
All rights reserved
Published by Our Sunday Visitor, Inc.
200 Noll Plaza, Huntington, Indiana 46750
Printed in the United States of America
Designed by James McIlrath
Library of Congress Catalog Card No. 81-82147
ISBN 0-87973-662-3

The First Christmas

by David Galusha
Illustrated by James McIlrath

OUR SUNDAY VISITOR, INC.
HUNTINGTON, INDIANA

A long time ago,
in a tiny village called Nazareth,
there lived a young woman named Mary.

Mary's mother, Anne, and her father, Joachim,
loved God very much.
They taught Mary to pray each day
and to be a kind and gentle person.

One day, while Mary was praying,
she was visited by an angel.
"Greetings, Mary," the angel said.
"God loves you very much."

The angel told Mary
that she was chosen to be
the mother of a very special child.
The child would be God's own Son.
The angel told Mary to name the child "Jesus."

Mary was engaged to marry a man named Joseph.
Joseph was a carpenter in the village of Nazareth.
He was known to be a very kind man
who loved God.

After Mary told him her wonderful news,
the angel came to Joseph and told him
that he too was chosen by God.
He and Mary were to become the family
into which Jesus was to be born.
Their strength and love
would be a model for all families.

Mary and Joseph were soon married.
They lived together in Joseph's home in Nazareth.
When it was almost time for Mary to give birth to Jesus,
she and Joseph had to start out on a long trip
to the town of Bethlehem.

The Emperor had ordered
that the number of people in the empire be counted.
Husbands were to take their families
to their home towns for the counting.
Bethlehem was Joseph's home town.
On the journey to Bethlehem,
Mary rode on a donkey
while Joseph walked alongside.

The journey to Bethlehem took a long time
and was especially difficult for Mary,
because her baby would soon be born.
Joseph wanted Mary to have a comfortable place to rest
when the baby was born.
But Bethlehem had only one hotel,
and when Mary and Joseph arrived there,
all the rooms were already filled with other travelers.

When the innkeeper found out
that Mary was about to have a baby,
he let Mary and Joseph stay in the stable,
where the animals were kept.
There, Joseph made beds of straw for Mary and himself.
He prepared a straw bed for the baby
in a manger used to hold food for the animals.

Tired from their journey,
Mary and Joseph lay down on their straw beds.
They were happy to have a place to stay.
They thanked God
for watching over them on their trip to Bethlehem.

The cows in the stable
and the donkey that had carried Mary
stood nearby.
The warmth of their bodies
and their gentle manner
helped Mary and Joseph feel welcome.

In the clear, quiet night,
the stars shone brightly over Bethlehem.
One place in the town
seemed especially bright and joyful.

It was the stable,
filled with the happiness of Mary and Joseph,
for Mary had given birth
to a beautiful baby boy—Jesus.
She wrapped the baby in the soft clothes
she had made for him.
Joseph laid the baby down
on the bed of straw in the manger.
Their hearts were filled with joy.

In the fields near Bethlehem,
there were shepherds watching over their sheep.
Some of the shepherds were awake,
listening to be sure the sheep were quiet and restful.
The other shepherds were sleeping peacefully.

Suddenly the shepherds were surrounded
by a bright light.
They were startled.
An angel spoke to them:
"Do not be afraid," the angel said.
"I am here to bring you good news.
In the town of Bethlehem
your Savior has been born this night.
You will find him in a stable,
sleeping in a manger."

Then the angel was joined by many other angels.
They were all singing:
"Glory to God in the highest.
Peace to all of good will."

The shepherds were very excited by the news
the angel had told them.
They hurried into Bethlehem
and found Mary and Joseph and Jesus in the stable.
They gathered around to see the baby
and to thank God for this wonderful night.

Meanwhile, in a far-off land,
there were three great kings
who were good and wise.
For many years they had been studying the stars
for signs of what the future would be.

One night they saw a star brighter than any other,
moving across the sky.
They had read about God's promise to send a Savior,
his own Son.
They believed that the bright star
was a sign that the Savior had been born.

So the three wise kings set out to follow the star.
They rode on camels in a long caravan,
with their families and their servants.
For many days they journeyed
over mountains and through fields.
They crossed parched desert lands.
Finally the star led them to Bethlehem.

In Bethlehem the wise kings found the place
where Mary and Joseph and Jesus were.
Like the shepherds,
the wise kings gathered around the baby.
They had brought him fine gifts
of gold, incense, and myrrh.
It seemed that all the world
had come to share in the joy
of that first Christmas night.